The All-American Book of Lists

MOUNTED INFORMATION NETWORK

W9-BUM-869

'DEC 5 2009

Chester
Library

DISCARD

250 West Main Street
Chester, NJ 07930

The All-American Book of Lists

A unique compendium of bizarre and fascinating facts from Alabama to Wyoming

Julian Ashe

ONEWORLD

OXFORD

A Oneworld Paperback Original

Published by Oneworld Publications 2009

Copyright © Julian Ashe 2009

The right of the Julian Ashe to be identified as the Author of this
work has been asserted by him in accordance with the Copyright,
Designs and Patents Act 1988

All rights reserved
Copyright under Berne Convention
A CIP record for this title is available
from the British Library

ISBN 978–1–85168–672–8

Typeset by Jayvee, Trivandrum, India
Cover design by D. R. Ink
Printed and bound in Great Britain by
Bell & Bain, Glasgow

Oneworld Publications
185 Banbury Road
Oxford OX2 7AR
England
www.oneworld-publications.com

Learn more about Oneworld. Join our mailing list to
find out about our latest titles and special offers at:

www.oneworld-publications.com

Contents

3 Lifestyle, Work, and Culture 52

8 Film and Television 123

Acknowledgments

Few books are written without the active support and opinions of others. I'd like to take this opportunity to thank my parents, Alan and Rosemarie Ashe, for their continued support and Samantha Wadkin for her encouragement and patience. I'd also like to thank my editor Mike Harpley for the opportunity, and for his guidance throughout this project.

Introduction

List-making introduces order. It prioritizes. It helps us understand. Distilling huge volumes of information into a straightforward, friendly format not only makes things easier; it casts a fascinating new light on the subject matter.

What better subject for a book of lists than the great country of America, so vast and so diverse that its facts – and its trivia – are endless? America loves its symbols: from the Bald Eagle of strength and courage, to the Liberty Bell of independence, the United States is ripe with fascinating facts.

America has achieved so much in its short history. In the late eighteenth century, its rivers saw the world's first steamboats; in 1903, the Wright Brothers were the first men to take to the air in a powered aircraft; it put the first man on the Moon in 1969; and in November 2008 elected its first African-American president – a huge achievement for a country where slavery lurks in its not-so-distant past. The lists in this book provide some remarkable insights into America's constantly evolving history.

Through hard work, persistence, and ingenuity, America has brought the world amazing inventions and technologies. The first floating bars of soap, the first milk bottles, the infamous Colt Six-Shooter, and the Harley Davidson are products of the American tradition of creativity and industry. The remarkable facts and statistics in the following pages provide an enthralling snapshot of that heritage.

The very geography of America embodies its extraordinary diversity. This is a country where temperatures range from a record -79°F in the Endicott Mountains of North Alaska to 134°F in Death Valley, California; a country that suffers more than a thousand tornadoes a year; a country that has 3,500,000 miles of rivers. These inventories cover the breadth of the United States, from the town of Boring, Oregon to the Presidential Palace in Washington DC (better known as the White House).

Much time and effort has gone into the research for this book. I hope you will enjoy reading it as much as I enjoyed discovering new and intriguing information. This is the ultimate American trivia guide and should provide ample mind-fodder for years to come.

I have tried hard to ensure that all the information is accurate. However, in a book with so many facts and figures, I'd be foolish to think there aren't some mistakes and some information that will change as time goes by. If you spot any errors or omissions, please contact the publisher.

So, are you all set to embark on a journey across this great country, past and present? Get ready to traverse the intriguing, the unbelievable, the surprising, and sometimes the downright bizarre!

Julian Ashe, May 2009

1

POLITICS AND GOVERNMENT

USA Fast Facts

Name	United States/USA/US/United States of America/America
Origin of name	Named after the Italian explorer, Amerigo Vespucci
Capital	Washington DC (population 591,833)
Currency	US Dollar ($)
Administrative divisions	50 Federal States (and 1 district)
Leading Industrial Sectors	Agriculture, Forestry, Fishing, Manufacturing, Mining, Construction, Finance

Gross Domestic Product	$13.84 trillion (2007)
Languages	82% English, 11% Spanish, 7% other
Largest cities (by population)	New York, Los Angeles, Chicago, Houston, Phoenix, Philadelphia
Population	308,824,640 (official 2008 estimate)
Religions	Protestant 51.3%, Catholic 23.9%, other Christians 1.6%, Mormon 1.7%, Jewish 1.7%, Buddhist 0.7%, Muslim 0.6%, Unaffiliated 12.1%, none 4%, rest unspecified

Ten Fascinating Facts

1 George Washington was the only president never to live in the White House. He died before the building was completed.

2 John Quincy Adams said his time as president was "the four most miserable years of my life."

3 Martin Van Buren was the first president to be born an American citizen.

4 James Buchanan was the only president to remain a bachelor all his life. His niece Harriet Lane served as his official White House hostess.

5 John Adams and Thomas Jefferson died on the same day (July 4, 1826, the 50th anniversary of the signing of the Declaration of Independence). President James Monroe also died on July 4, in 1831.

6   Grover Cleveland was a heavy smoker and was diagnosed with a malignant tumor of the mouth in 1893. It was feared this negative news could affect the economy so it was kept secret. Cleveland underwent an operation (on a yacht in the East River in New York) in which his upper jaw was removed along with the tumor. He was fitted with a rubber jaw, and spent months re-learning how to speak naturally. The American public didn't learn of the secret until 1917.

7   Franklin D Roosevelt and his wife Eleanor were fifth cousins. FDR was also a fourth cousin of Presidents Ulysses S Grant and Zachary Taylor, a fifth cousin of President Theodore Roosevelt, and a seventh cousin of Winston Churchill.

8   Harry S Truman liked routine. He rose at five each morning, took a two-mile walk around Washington, had a shot of bourbon, a massage, and a light breakfast, before setting off to the Oval Office. He was always at his desk by 7AM.

9   John F Kennedy suffered from serious back pain and regularly wore a back brace, including on the day he was shot in Dallas. This kept him upright after the first shot to his neck; it's possible that without the brace, he might have slumped forward and avoided the second, fatal, shot to his head.

10   Ronald Reagan had a piece of suspicious tissue removed from his nose in 1985. To avoid leaks, the sample was sent for biopsy under the name of Ms Tracy Malone. The results came back negative and the White House was able to issue a statement declaring that no further treatment was necessary.

Presidents

1 George Washington (No political party)
April 1789 to March 1797

2 John Adams (Federalist)
March 1797 to March 1801

3 Thomas Jefferson (Democratic-Republicans)
March 1801 to March 1809

4 James Madison (Democratic-Republicans)
March 1809 to March 1817

5 James Monroe (Democratic-Republicans)
March 1817 to March 1825

6 John Quincy Adams (Democratic-Republicans/
National Republican)
March 1825 to March 1829

7 Andrew Jackson (Democratic)
March 1829 to March 1837

8 Martin Van Buren (Democratic)
March 1837 to March 1841

9 William Henry Harrison (Whig)
March 1841 to April 1841

10 John Tyler (Whig/No party (expelled from the party during his presidency))
April 1841 to March 1845

11 James Polk (Democratic)
March 1845 to March 1849

12 Zachary Taylor (Whig)
March 1849 to July 1850

13 Millard Fillmore (Whig)
July 1850 to March 1853

14 Franklin Pierce (Democratic)
March 1853 to March 1857

15 James Buchanan (Democratic)
March 1857 to March 1861

16 Abraham Lincoln (Republican National Union)
March 1861 to April 1865

17 Andrew Johnson (Democratic National Union)
April 1865 to March 1869

18 Ulysses S Grant (Republican)
March 1869 to March 1877

19 Rutherford B Hayes (Republican)
March 1877 to March 1881

20 James A Garfield (Republican)
March 1881 to September 1881

21 Chester Arthur (Republican)
September 1881 to March 1885

22 Grover Cleveland (Democratic)
March 1885 to March 1889

23 Benjamin Harrison (Republican)
March 1889 to March 1893

24   Grover Cleveland (Democratic)
March 1893 to March 1897

25   William McKinley (Republican)
March 1897 to September 1901

26   Theodore Roosevelt (Republican)
September 1901 to March 1909

27   William Howard Taft (Republican)
September 1909 to March 1913

28   Woodrow Wilson (Democratic)
March 1913 to March 1921

29   Warren Harding (Republican)
March 1921 to August 1923

30   Calvin Coolidge (Republican)
August 1923 to March 1929

31   Herbert Hoover (Republican)
March 1929 to March 1933

32   Franklin D Roosevelt (Democratic)
March 1933 to April 1945

33   Harry S Truman (Democratic)
April 1945 to January 1953

34   Dwight Eisenhower (Republican)
January 1953 to January 1961

35   John F Kennedy (Democratic)
January 1961 to November 1963

36   Lyndon B Johnson (Democratic)
November 1963 to January 1969

37   Richard Nixon (Republican)
January 1969 to August 1974

38   Gerald Ford (Republican)
August 1974 to January 1977

39   Jimmy Carter (Democratic)
January 1977 to January 1981

40   Ronald Reagan (Republican)
January 1981 to January 1989

41   George H W Bush (Republican)
January 1989 to January 1993

42   William Clinton (Democratic)
January 1993 to January 2001

43   George W Bush (Republican)
January 2001 to January 2009

44   Barack H Obama (Democratic)
January 2009

Political Records

 The longest inaugural address in American History was given by President William Henry Harrison (one hour and forty-five minutes). The shortest was given by George Washington at his second inauguration (133 words).

 In 1811, at 32 years old, Joseph Story was the youngest person ever to serve in the Supreme Court.

President Theodore Roosevelt was the first president to travel outside the country while in office. He visited Panama to review the construction of the Panama Canal (1906).

 John Tyler was the first vice-president to succeed a president who died in office. He was also the only president to commit treason.

 Thomas Jefferson Boynton was 25 years old when he became the youngest Federal judge, in the Southern District of Florida in 1863.

 In 1880, James Garfield became the first presidential candidate to spend more than one million dollars on his campaign.

 Grover Cleveland was the first president to serve two non-consecutive terms (first elected in 1885 and re-elected in 1893).

 The first female cabinet member was Frances Perkins, who served as Secretary of Labor for twelve years from 1933, under Franklin D Roosevelt.

 James A Garfield was the only ordained preacher ever to be elected president. He was a minister of the Church of the Disciples of Christ.

The Constitution

 The American Constitution is the oldest and shortest written constitution in the world.

Fifty-five delegates attended the Constitutional Convention in 1787, at which the constitution was drafted.

 The Constitution passed into law in 1788.

 "Pensylvania" is spelt incorrectly in the Constitution.

 Jacob Shallus, Clerk to the General Assembly, actually wrote the text of the Constitution.

 Constitution Day is celebrated on September 17, the date the framers signed the document.

 The oldest person to sign the Constitution was Benjamin Franklin (81 years).

The youngest person to sign it was Jonathan Dayton of New Jersey (26 years).

 At the time of signing, the population of the United States was approximately 4 million.

The Constitution is preserved and displayed at the National Archives in Washington DC

The Senate and Senators

The Senate has 100 members (two from each state).

Senators must be 30 years old (when seated, not elected).

 Senators must be United States' citizens for at least nine years before election.

 John Eaton was the youngest-ever senator, just 28 years old at his swearing-in in 1818. Even though he was below the legal age limit when he started, he served until 1829.

 Strom Thurmond was the oldest senator, celebrating his 100th birthday while in office.

 The first radio broadcast from the Senate Chamber was in March 1929.

 The first television broadcast was in December 1974.

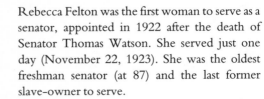 Rebecca Felton was the first woman to serve as a senator, appointed in 1922 after the death of Senator Thomas Watson. She served just one day (November 22, 1923). She was the oldest freshman senator (at 87) and the last former slave-owner to serve.

 Hattie Caraway was the first woman elected as senator (in 1932).

 Hiram Revels was the first African-American elected as senator (1870).

 James Monroe was the first former senator to be elected president (1816).

Hillary Clinton was the first former First Lady to be elected as senator (2001).

Four senators have received the Nobel Peace Prize (Elihu Root in 1912, Frank Billings Kellogg in 1929, Cordell Hull in 1945 and Albert Arnold (Al) Gore in 2007).

Elections

November was chosen as election month because in the eighteenth century, America was a predominantly agrarian society. In November, the harvest was over, and country-dwellers had time to travel to the poll.

Tuesday was chosen as Election Day (in 1845) to allow people in rural communities time to travel to the polling stations on foot or by horse while avoiding travel on the Sabbath.

Election Day is a legal holiday in Delaware, Hawaii, Kentucky, Montana, New Jersey, New York, Ohio, and West Virginia.

Ronald Reagan won the highest-ever number of Electoral College votes (525, in 1984).

Nixon and Reagan won the most states (in 1972 and 1984 respectively): 49.

Norman Thomas, of the Socialist Party, ran for office most times (1928, 1932, 1936, 1940, 1944, and 1948).

The maximum an individual can contribute towards a federal election is $2,300.

 The 2008 election was the first time that the two candidates raised more than $1 billion from all sources.

 Barack Obama was the first African-American to be elected president, in 2008.

Barack Obama

 First African-American president

 First Hawaii-born president (Honolulu)

 Third president from Illinois

 Obama's father, a government economist, was Kenyan, of the Luo ethnic group

 In Swahili, "Barack" means "one who is blessed"

 Left-handed – sixth post-war presidential south-paw

 Owns a pair of red boxing gloves signed by Muhammad Ali

Can speak Spanish

Was called "Barry" as a child; began using his full name at university

Rarely drinks alcohol and doesn't drink coffee

 Reportedly keeps a carving of a wooden hand holding an egg on his desk; a Kenyan symbol of the frailty of life

Civil War Veterans who Became President

 Andrew Johnson (1865–1869): Brigadier General (Volunteer Regiment); succeeded Lincoln on his assassination in April 1865.

 Ulysses S Grant (1869–1877): Lieutenant-Colonel (Volunteer Regiment), later General (1866). Resigned in 1869 to become president.

 Rutherford B Hayes (1877–1881): Major (23 Ohio), later Brigadier General. Elected to Congress in 1864, became president in 1877.

 James A Garfield (1881): Lieutenant Colonel (42 Ohio), later Major General (Volunteer Regiment). Elected to Congress in 1862, became president in 1881.

 Chester A Arthur (1881–1885): Assistant Quartermaster-General (New York Militia), later Major General. Became president in 1881.

 Benjamin Harrison (1889–1893): Second Lieutenant (70 Indiana), later Brigadier General. Left the army in 1865 to resume his law practice;

became president in 1889. Great-grandson of Benjamin Harrison, one of the signatories of the Declaration of Independence.

 William McKinley (1897–1901): Private (Company E, 23 Ohio), later Brevet Major. Became president in 1897.

Last Words

John Adams	"Thomas Jefferson still survives."
Thomas Jefferson	"Is it the fourth?" (July 4, 1826)
Andrew Jackson	"Oh, do not cry. Be good children, and we shall all meet in heaven."
William Henry Harrison	"I wish you to understand the true principles of government. I wish them carried out. I ask nothing more."
John Tyler	"Doctor, I am going. Perhaps it is best."
Zachary Taylor	"I am about to die. I expect the summons very soon. I have tried to discharge my duties faithfully. I regret nothing, but I am sorry that I am about to leave my friends."
Ulysses S Grant	"Water!"

Rutherford B Hayes	"I know that I am going where Lucy is."
James A Garfield	"Swaim, can't you stop this? (assassinated) Oh, Swaim!"
Grover Cleveland	"I have tried so hard to do right."
William McKinley	"Goodbye, goodbye to all. It is God's will. His will, not ours, be done."
Theodore Roosevelt	"Please put out the light."
Warren G Harding	"That's good. Go on, read some more."
Franklin D Roosevelt	"I have a terrific headache."
Dwight D Eisenhower	"I want to go, God take me!"

Burial Places

1 Washington
Mount Vernon, Virginia

2 Adams, J
Quincy, Massachusetts

3 Jefferson
Charlottesville, Virginia

4 Madison
Montpelier Station, Virginia

5 Monroe
Richmond, Virginia

6	Adams, JQ Quincy, Massachusetts
7	Jackson Nashville, Tennessee
8	Van Buren Kinderhook, New York
9	Harrison North Bend, Ohio
10	Tyler Richmond, Virginia
11	Polk Nashville, Tennessee
12	Taylor Louisville, Kentucky
13	Fillmore Buffalo, New York
14	Pierce Concord, New Hampshire
15	Buchanan Lancaster, Pennsylvania
16	Lincoln Springfield, Illinois
17	Johnson, A Greeneville, Tennessee
18	Grant New York, New York

19	Hayes
	Fremont, Ohio

20	Garfield
	Cleveland, Ohio

21	Arthur
	Albany, New York

22	Cleveland
	Princeton, New Jersey

23	McKinley
	Canton, Ohio

24	Roosevelt, T
	Oyster Bay, New York

25	Taft
	Arlington National Cemetery, Washington DC

26	Wilson
	Washington National Cathedral, Washington DC

27	Harding
	Marion, Ohio

28	Coolidge
	Plymouth, Vermont

29	Hoover
	West Branch, Iowa

30	Roosevelt, FD
	Hyde Park, New York

31	Truman
	Independence, Missouri

Presidential Quotes

"To be prepared for war is one of the most effectual means of preserving peace."

George Washington

"The happiness of society is the end of government."

John Adams

"The problem to be solved is, not what form of government is perfect, but which of the forms is least imperfect?"

James Madison

"An honorable defeat is better than a dishonorable victory."

Millard Fillmore

"The ballot box is the surest arbiter of disputes among free men."

James Buchanan

"If slavery is not wrong, nothing is wrong."

Abraham Lincoln

"I have never advocated war except as a means of peace."

Ulysses S Grant

"He serves his party best who serves the country best."

Rutherford Hayes

"Men may die, but the fabric of our free institutions remains unshaken."

Chester Alan Arthur

"Above all, tell the truth."

Stephen Grover Cleveland

"The only man who makes no mistake is the man who does nothing."

Theodore Roosevelt

"A good leader can't get too far ahead of his followers."

Franklin D Roosevelt

"America is best described by one word: freedom."
Dwight D Eisenhower

"Absolute freedom of the press to discuss public questions is a foundation stone of American liberty."
Herbert Hoover

"You cannot stop the spread of an idea by passing a law against it."
Harry S Truman

"A pessimist is one who makes difficulties of his opportunities and an optimist is one who makes opportunities of his difficulties."
Harry S Truman

"And so my fellow Americans, ask not what your country can do for you; ask what you can do for your country."
John F Kennedy

"Truth is the glue that holds governments together. Compromise is the oil that makes governments go."
Gerald R Ford

"I like the job I have, but if I had to live my life over again, I would like to have ended up a sports writer."
Richard M Nixon

"America is too great for small dreams."
Ronald Reagan

"If anyone tells you that America's best days are
behind her, they're looking the wrong way."

George HW Bush

The White House

★ By Act of Congress, signed by Washington in
1790, the Federal Government resides in a district "not exceeding ten miles square, on the
river Potomac."

★ Postal address is 1600 Pennsylvania Avenue.

★ Designed by Irish-born architect James Hoban,
winner of a competition to find a design for the
"President's House."

★ Building began in 1792. Sandstone and wood
came from Virginia and North Carolina and
bricks were made on the North Lawn.
Stonemasons were brought in from Scotland.

★ Has suffered two fires: One caused by the
British in 1814 and another in the West Wing in
1929.

 Has 6 levels, 132 rooms, 35 bathrooms, 412
doors, 147 windows, 28 fireplaces, 8 staircases,
and 3 elevators.

 Welcomes approximately 6,000 visitors a day.

Has been known as the "President's Palace," the "President's House," and the "Executive Mansion." President Theodore Roosevelt officially named it "The White House" in 1901.

 Kitchen has five full-time chefs, who can cater for 140 dinner guests and up to 1,000 for canapés.

 Takes 570 gallons of paint to cover the outside.

 Has a tennis court, jogging track, swimming pool, movie theater, and bowling lane.

Symbols

Great Seal	Features the American bald eagle. Designed by request of Continental Congress, approved in 1782.
Flag	Thirteen red and white stripes represent the first thirteen colonies; fifty white stars on a blue field – one for each state.
Bald Eagle	National bird, representing strength, courage, and independence.
Uncle Sam	Personification of the United States, often shown as an elderly man dressed in the colors of the American flag. First use dates back to the War of 1812.

Pledge of Allegiance	Oath of loyalty to the country. Recited standing to attention, facing the flag and with the right hand held over the heart.
National Anthem	Star Spangled Banner: Originated from a popular drinking song of the early 1800s.
National Motto	"In God We Trust:" first appeared in coin in 1864; confirmed as the official motto in 1956.
Statue of Liberty	Located on Liberty Island in New York; represents a woman escaping the chains of tyranny (the broken remains lie at her feet). Formally known as "Liberty Enlightening the World."
Liberty Bell	Bell of Independence, originally rung on July 8, 1776, in Philadelphia to proclaim the independence of the United States of America from the British.

Dollar Bills

Note: Some notes are no longer produced but are still legal tender.

 One Dollar – George Washington: First president, led the Continental Army to victory over the British in the American War of Independence.

Two Dollar – Thomas Jefferson: Third president, one of the principal authors of the Declaration of Independence.

 Five Dollar – Abraham Lincoln: Sixteenth president, led the country through the Civil War. Assassinated as the war was coming to an end.

 Ten Dollar – Alexander Hamilton: First Secretary of the Treasury; economist and political philosopher.

 Twenty Dollar – Andrew Jackson: Seventh president; commander of the American forces at the Battle of New Orleans.

 Fifty Dollar – Ulysses S Grant: Eighteenth president; achieved international fame as the leading Union general in the American Civil War.

 One Hundred Dollar – Benjamin Franklin: Founding father of the United States; leading author, politician, printer, inventor, and scientist.

 Five Hundred Dollar – William McKinley: Twenty-fifth president; last Civil War veteran to be elected.

 One Thousand Dollar – Grover Cleveland: Twenty-second and twenty-fourth president; only president to serve two non-consecutive terms.

Five Thousand – James Madison: Fourth president. Considered "Father of the Constitution;" one of its principal authors.

Ten Thousand – Salmon P Chase: Leading American politician and jurist in the American Civil War. Treasury Secretary under Abraham Lincoln and Chief Justice of the United States.

Washington DC Memorials and Landmarks

Arlington National Cemetery	Located in Virginia, on the Potomac, directly opposite Washington DC. Became a military cemetery in 1864. Covers more than 600 acres. Resting-place of more than 240,000 service personnel and their relatives. In 1921, an unknown soldier of World War I was buried there; the monument of the Tomb of the Unknown Soldier was opened to the public in 1932.
Capitol	Home of Congress. Sited at the eastern end of the National Mall; most recognizable feature is the 180-foot high cast iron Dome of the Great Rotunda.
Jefferson Memorial	Based on the design of the Roman Pantheon. Jefferson was third president of the United States, famous for drafting the Declaration of Independence, and regarded as the political philosopher of the American Revolution.

Lincoln Memorial	In honor of Lincoln's (sixteenth president) contribution to American politics, modeled on a Greek (Doric) temple, completed in 1922. Has three chambers: the central one houses the well-known marble statue of Lincoln; the Gettysburg address and Lincoln's second inaugural address are carved on the walls of the other two.
National Archives	On Constitution Avenue, the official library where the records of the three branches of the US government are kept. The Declaration of Independence, the Constitution, and Bill of Rights are on display.
National Mall	Lawn, 146 acres, extending from the Potomac River to the Capitol Building. Site of political rallies and festivals, surrounded by memorials and various branches of the Smithsonian Institution.
Smithsonian Institution	Ten branches of the Smithsonian surround the National Mall, including the National Air and Space Museum, the Museum of National History, and the National Portrait Gallery. Named for Smithson, an eccentric and wealthy Englishman, who, although he had never been to America, left money, his scientific library, and his collection of

	minerals to create a museum in Washington DC.
Holocaust Memorial Museum	National institution for the documentation, study, and interpretation of Holocaust history. Opened in 1993, costing more than $168 million.
Vietnam Veterans Memorial	Honors the men and women who died in the Vietnam War. More than 58,000 names are etched on the memorial.
Washington Memorial	Obelisk, covered with white marble; stands just over 555 feet high. Memorial stones from the 50 states, foreign countries, and various organizations line the inside walls. The top of the monument can be reached by elevator.
White House	Official residence of the president. Site chosen by President George Washington in 1792. Public functions are held on the first floor and the second and third floors are the family residence of the president.
World War II Memorial	Commemorates the millions of Americans who served in World War II, the more than 400,000 soldiers who died, and the millions who supported the war effort from home.

Want to be an FBI Agent?

Some questions you might be asked in your application:

 Have you ever been fired?

 Did you register with the Selective Service System as required?

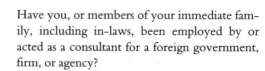 What foreign countries have you visited?

Have you, or members of your immediate family, including in-laws, been employed by or acted as a consultant for a foreign government, firm, or agency?

 Have you engaged in acts or activities designed to overthrow the United States government by force?

 Have you ever been over 120 days delinquent on any debt or had any debt placed for collection?

 Are you a licensed motorcycle driver?

Where was your sister's spouse born?

Are you now, or have you ever been, a member of a foreign or domestic organization, association, movement, group, or combination of persons that is totalitarian, fascist, communist, or subversive?

Are you aware of any information about yourself or anyone with whom you are or have been closely associated (including relatives and roommates) that tends to reflect unfavorably on your reputation, morals, character, abilities, or loyalty to the United States?

 If appointed as a Special Agent, do you agree to serve a minimum of three years, and do you clearly understand that you must be available for an assignment wherever your services are needed?

 Do you use alcohol? To what extent?

 Have you or any member of your family ever suffered from, or been treated for, any form of mental illness, insanity, epilepsy, been mentally retarded, or had psychiatric consultation of any kind?

 Do you have any physical defects, including any which would preclude unrestricted, regular participation in all phases of the Bureau's firearms training, physical training, and defensive tactics?

★ Have you ever been declared bankrupt?

★ How did you become interested in Bureau employment?

2

STATES

Ten Fascinating Facts

1   Alaska has the longest coastline of any state – approximately 6,640 miles.

2   Arkansas has the only active diamond mine in the US.

3   California has the largest county by area, San Bernardino County (nearly three million acres) and the largest county by population (Los Angeles, 9.2 million).

4   Delaware was the first state to ratify the Constitution (1787).

5   The Hawaiian Islands are the result of the eruption of underwater volcanoes between 375,000 and 65 million years ago.

6   Idaho has the longest main street in the US – 33 miles, in Island Park.

7   Maine is the only state whose name has just one syllable.

8   New Mexico's capital (Santa Fe) is the highest capital city in the US: approximately 7,000 feet above sea level.

9   Utah was acquired by the United States in the treaty that ended the Mexican War.

10   Yellowstone, Wyoming was the first official national park to be created.

Physical Features

Total surface area	3,718,710 square miles (land 3,537,436 square miles; water 181,274 square miles)
Width	2,680 miles
Length	1,582 miles
Most northerly point	Point Barrow, Alaska
Most southerly point (US territory)	Rose Atoll, American Samoa
Most southerly point (US states)	Ka Lae, Hawaii
Most easterly point (US territories)	Point Udall, St Croix, US Virgin Islands

Most easterly point (US states)	Sail Rock, West Quoddy Head, Maine
Most westerly point (US territories)	Udall Point, Guam
Most westerly point (US states)	Cape Wrangell, Attu Island, Alaska
Geographical center (continental US)	Two miles north-west of Lebanon, Kansas
Geographical center (including Hawaii and Alaska)	Near Belle Fourche, South Dakota
Highest point	Mount McKinley, Alaska (20,320 ft)
Lowest point	Death Valley, California (–282 ft)
Most distant points	Log Point, Elliot Key, Florida and Kure Island, Hawaii

Extreme Weather

 Highest-ever temperature: 134°F, Death Valley, California, 1913

 Lowest-ever temperature: –79.8°F, Prospect Creek Camp, Endicott Mountains, Alaska, 1971

 Highest-ever surface wind speed: 231 mph, Mount Washington, New Hampshire, 1934

Longest rain-free period: 767 days between 1912 and 1914, Baghdad, California

 Record rainfall: 12 inches in just 42 minutes, June 1947, Holt, Missouri

 Highest ultraviolet exposure: Florida (more than one hundred times Maine's)

 Hottest year: 2007, more than 8,000 new heat records

 Tornadoes: More than 1,000 tornadoes a year

Damage: 78 weather-related disasters since the 1970s in which overall costs have exceeded $1 billion

Highest Mountains

(contiguous states)

 Mt Whitney, California: 14,494 ft

Mt Elbert, Colorado: 14,433 ft

Mt Massive, Colorado: 14,421 ft

Mt Harvard, Colorado: 14,420 ft

Mt Rainier, Washington: 14,410 ft

Mt Williamson, California: 14,375 ft

Longest Rivers

★ Missouri: 2,540 miles

★ Mississippi: 2,340 miles

★ Yukon: 1,980 miles

★ Rio Grande: 1,900 miles

★ St Lawrence: 1,900 miles

★ Arkansas: 1,460 miles

★ Colorado: 1,450 miles

★ Atchafalaya: 1,420 miles

★ Ohio: 1,310 miles

★ Red: 1,290 miles

★ Brazos: 1,280 miles

★ Columbia: 1,240 miles

★ Snake: 1,040 miles

River Trivia

Number of rivers	More than 250,000
Total river length	Over 3,500,000 miles

Largest river	Mississippi; flows at 593,000 cubic feet per second at its mouth
Most biodiversity	Cahaba River, Alabama; approximately 131 different species of fish
Only state bordered by two navigable rivers	Iowa (Missouri and Mississippi)
Most urban river	Charles River, Massachusetts; flows through 23 towns and cities in its 80-mile length
Oldest river	New River, North Carolina
Deepest river gorge	Hell's Canyon, Oregon; 8,000 ft deep

Largest States (by area)

★ Alaska: 663,267 sq miles

★ Texas: 268,581 sq miles

★ California: 163,696 sq miles

★ Montana: 147,042 sq miles

★ New Mexico: 121,589 sq miles

★ Arizona: 113,998 sq miles

★ Nevada: 110,561 sq miles

★ Colorado: 104,094 sq miles

Largest States (by population)

★ California: 36,553,215

★ Texas: 23,904,380

★ New York: 19,297,729

★ Florida: 18,251,243

★ Illinois: 12,852,548

★ Pennsylvania: 12,432,792

★ Ohio: 11,466,917

★ Michigan: 10,071,822

Time Zones

AST	Atlantic Standard Time	GMT –4
ADT	Atlantic Daylight Time	GMT –3
EST	Eastern Standard Time	GMT –5
EDT	Eastern Daylight Time	GMT –4

CST	Central Standard Time	GMT -6
CDT	Central Daylight Time	GMT -5
MST	Mountain Standard Time	GMT -7
MDT	Mountain Daylight Time	GMT -6
PST	Pacific Standard Time	GMT -8
PDT	Pacific Daylight Time	GMT -7
AKST	Alaska Standard Time	GMT -9
AKDT	Alaska Daylight Time	GMT -8
HAST	Hawaii-Aleutian Standard Time	GMT -10
HADT	Hawaii-Aleutian Daylight Time	GMT -9

Origin of State Names

ALABAMA	Named after local Native American tribe
ALASKA	Aleut word meaning "great land" or "main land"
ARIZONA	Probably from the Spanish "arizonac" (good oak)
ARKANSAS	From the Algonquian dialect
CALIFORNIA	From the Spanish "cali for- nia" (hot as an oven)
COLORADO	From the Spanish "ruddy" or "red," referring to the Colorado river

CONNECTICUT	From a Quinnehtukqut word meaning "beside the long river"
DELAWARE	Named for Sir Thomas West, 12th Baron De La Warr
FLORIDA	From the Spanish "florido" (flowery)
GEORGIA	Named in honor of King George II of Great Britain
HAWAII	Either from "hawa" (home-land) and "ii" (small) or from "hawaiki" (place of the gods)
IDAHO	Possibly a variation of the Kiowa-Apache word "idaahe" (enemy)
ILLINOIS	Named after the indigenous Ilinouek people
INDIANA	"The land of the Indians"
IOWA	Named for the Ioway tribe
KANSAS	Sioux word meaning "people of the south wind"
KENTUCKY	From the Iroquoian word "kentahteh" (tomorrow, the coming day)
LOUISIANA	Named in honor of King Louis XIV of France

MAINE	Possible reference to the province of Mayne in France or simply from the English "mainland"
MARYLAND	Named in honor of Queen Henrietta Maria, wife of King Charles I
MASSACHUSETTS	From the name of the indigenous Massachusett people, meaning "at or about the great hill"
MICHIGAN	From the Ojibwe "mis-shikama" (big lake)
MINNESOTA	From the Dakota "mnisota" (sky-colored water)
MISSISSIPPI	From "messipi" (Father of the waters or great waters)
MISSOURI	Named after the Missouri tribe
MONTANA	From the Spanish "montana" (mountain)
NEBRASKA	From an Oto tribe word meaning "flat river"
NEVADA	From the Spanish "nevada" (snow-covered)
NEW HAMPSHIRE	Named after Hampshire (English county)

NEW JERSEY	Named after the Channel Island of Jersey
NEW MEXICO	May refer to the Aztec God "Mexitli"
NEW YORK	Named in honor of the Duke of York
NORTH CAROLINA	Named after King Charles I of Great Britain, from "Carolus," the Latin form of Charles
NORTH DAKOTA	Named after the Dakota, a Sioux tribe
OHIO	Either from a Wyandot word meaning "large" or "the great one," or the Iroquoian "beautiful river"
OKLAHOMA	From two Choctaw words "ukla" and "huma" (red person)
OREGON	Unknown; first recorded in 1778 in the letters of Maj. Robert Rogers
PENNSYLVANIA	From the Latin for Penn's Woods, in honor of Admiral Penn
RHODE ISLAND	Named after the Greek island of Rhodes

SOUTH CAROLINA	Named after the King Charles I of Great Britain
SOUTH DAKOTA	Named after the Dakota, a Sioux tribe
TENNESSEE	May refer to Native American villages known as "Tanasqui"
TEXAS	From the Caddoan word "teysha" (friend or ally)
UTAH	From a Navajo word "yut-tahih" (people who are higher)
VERMONT	Probably an English version of the French "verts monts" (green mountains)
VIRGINIA	Named after the "Virgin Queen," Queen Elizabeth I of England
WASHINGTON	Named in honor of George Washington
WEST VIRGINIA	Named after Queen Elizabeth I of England
WISCONSIN	Possibly from the native word "miskwasiniing" (red stone)
WYOMING	From the Delaware word "mecheweami-ing" (on the big flat river)

State Mottos

Alabama	We dare to defend our rights
Alaska	North to the future
Arizona	God enriches
Arkansas	Let the people rule
California	I have found it
Colorado	Nothing without providence
Connecticut	He who transplanted still sustains
Delaware	Liberty and independence
District of Columbia	Justice to all
Florida	In God we trust
Georgia	Wisdom, justice, and moderation
Hawaii	The life of the land is perpetuated by righteousness
Idaho	May she endure forever
Illinois	State sovereignty: national union
Indiana	The cross-roads of America
Iowa	Our liberties we prize and our rights we will maintain
Kansas	To the stars through difficulties

Kentucky	United we stand, divided we fall
Louisiana	Union, justice, and confidence
Maine	I lead
Maryland	Strong deeds, gentle words
Massachusetts	By the sword we seek peace, but peace only under liberty
Michigan	If you seek a pleasant peninsula, look around you
Minnesota	The star of the north
Mississippi	By valor and arms
Missouri	The welfare of the people shall be the supreme law
Montana	Gold and silver
Nebraska	Equality before the law
Nevada	All for our country
New Hampshire	Live free or die
New Jersey	Liberty and prosperity
New Mexico	It grows as it goes
New York	Ever upward
North Carolina	To be rather than seem
North Dakota	Liberty and union, now and forever, one and inseparable
Ohio	With God, all things are possible

Oklahoma	Work conquers all
Oregon	She flies with her own wings
Pennsylvania	Virtue, liberty, and independence
Rhode Island	Hope
South Carolina	Prepared in mind and resources/ While I breathe I hope
South Dakota	Under God the people rule
Tennessee	Agriculture and commerce
Texas	Friendship
Utah	Industry
Vermont	Freedom and unity
Virginia	Thus always to tyrants
Washington	By and by
West Virginia	Mountaineers are always free
Wisconsin	Forward
Wyoming	Equal rights

State Nicknames

Alabama	Yellowhammer State
Alaska	The Last Frontier
Arizona	Grand Canyon State

Arkansas	Natural State
California	Golden State
Connecticut	Constitution State
Colorado	Centennial State
Delaware	First State/Diamond State
Florida	Sunshine State
Georgia	Peach State
Hawaii	Aloha State
Idaho	Gem State
Illinois	Prairie State/Land of Lincoln
Indiana	Hoosier State
Iowa	Hawkeye State
Kansas	Sunflower State
Kentucky	Bluegrass State
Louisiana	Pelican State
Maine	Pine Tree State
Maryland	Old Line State
Massachusetts	Bay State/Colony State
Michigan	Great Lakes State
Minnesota	North Star State
Mississippi	Magnolia State
Missouri	Show-Me State

Montana	Treasure State
Nebraska	Cornhusker State
Nevada	Silver State
New Hampshire	Granite State
New Jersey	Garden State
New Mexico	Land of Enchantment
New York	Empire State
North Carolina	Tar Heel State/Old North State
North Dakota	Peace Garden State
Ohio	Buckeye State
Oklahoma	Sooner State
Oregon	Beaver State
Pennsylvania	Keystone State
Rhode Island	Ocean State
South Carolina	Palmetto State
South Dakota	Mount Rushmore State
Tennessee	Volunteer State
Texas	Lone Star State
Utah	Beehive State
Vermont	Green Mountain State
Virginia	The Old Dominion
Washington	Evergreen State

West Virginia	Mountain State
Wisconsin	Badger State
Wyoming	Equality State

Most Populous Cities

★ New York, New York: 8,214,426

★ Los Angeles, California: 3,849,378

★ Chicago, Illinois: 2,833,321

★ Houston, Texas: 2,144,491

★ Phoenix, Arizona: 1,512,986

★ Philadelphia, Pennsylvania: 1,448,934

★ San Antonio, Texas: 1,296,682

★ San Diego, California: 1,256,951

★ Dallas, Texas: 1,232,940

City Firsts

★ Lighthouse: Boston, Massachusetts, 1716

★ Opera House: New Orleans, Louisiana, 1859

★ Ambulance Service: Cincinnati, Ohio, 1865

★ Zoological Garden: Philadelphia, Pennsylvania, 1874

★ Traffic Lights: Cleveland, Ohio, 1914

Most Self-satisfied Town Names

★ Beauty, Kentucky

★ Best, Texas

★ Carefree, Arizona

★ Celebration, Florida

★ Friendly, West Virginia

★ Happy Camp, California

★ Happyland, Connecticut

★ Happy Hills, Massachusetts

★ Happy Valley, Hawaii

★ Ideal, Georgia

★ Lovely, Kentucky

★ Luck Stop, Kentucky

★ Paradise, Michigan

★ Smileyberg, Kansas

★ Success, Missouri

Towns Worth Avoiding?

★ Boring, Oregon

★ Eek, Alaska

★ Embarrass, Wisconsin

★ Frankenstein, Missouri

★ Greasy, Oklahoma

★ Gripe, Arizona

★ Hell, Michigan

★ Oddville, Kentucky

★ Peculiar, Missouri

★ Slaughterville, Oklahoma

★ Sod, West Virginia

Towns You Could Eat?

★ Big Rock Candy Mountain, Vermont

★ Buttermilk, Kansas

★ Candy Town, Ohio

★ Cheesequake, New Jersey

★ Chocolate Bayou, Texas

★ Goodfood, Mississippi

★ Ham Lake, Minnesota

★ Oatmeal, Texas

★ Oniontown, Pennsylvania

★ Picnic, Florida

★ Pie Town, New Mexico

★ Sandwich, Massachusetts

★ Spuds, Florida

★ Sugar City, Idaho

★ Toast, North Carolina

★ Tortilla Flat, Arizona

Animal Town Names

★ Bear, Delaware

★ Dinosaur, Colorado

★ Goat Town, Georgia

★ Gray Mule, Texas

★ Hippo, Kentucky

★ Hungry Horse, Montana

★ Lame Deer, Montana

★ Mammoth, West Virginia

★ Sleeping Buffalo, Montana

★ Trout, Louisiana

★ Viper, Kentucky

3

Lifestyle, Work, and Culture

Social Characteristics (2006)

Average household size	2.61
Average family size	3.20
Total population	299,398,485
Male	147,434,940
Female	151,963,545
Median age	36.4
Under 5 years	20,385,773
Over 18 years	225,633,342
Over 65 years	37,191,004

Labor force	152,193,214
Median travel time to work	25 minutes
Median household income	$48,451
Per capita income	$25,267
Single race	293,285,839 (98%)
White	221,331,507
Hispanic/Latino	44,252,278
Black/African-American	37,051,483
Asian	13,100,095
Native American/Alaska Native	2,369,431
Native Hawaiian/Pacific Islander	426,194
Other	19,007,129

Ins and Outs

 One birth every 8 seconds

 One death every 12 seconds

 One international immigrant every 27 seconds

 One American native emigrant every 100 seconds

One birth every 8 seconds Net gain of one person every 12 seconds

1900 to 2000

	1900	2000
Adults completing high school	15%	83%
Average annual income (in 1999 dollars)	$8,620	$23,812
Average size of household	4.76	2.62
Average working week	60 hours	44 hours
Beer consumption	58.8 gallons per adult	31.6 gallons per adult
Most immigrants from	Austria-Hungary	Mexico
Books published	6,356	65,800
Cars produced	5,000	5,500,500
Cigarettes produced	4 billion	720 billion
Most millionaires per capita	Buffalo, NY	Seattle, WA
Deaths in childbirth	0.9%	0.01%
Deaths from industrial accidents	35,000	6,100
Defense expenditure (in 1999 dollars)	$4 billion	$268 billion
Divorced men	0.3%	8.2%

Divorced women	0.5%	10.3%
Dow Jones Industrial Average	68.13	11,000
Farm population	29,875,000	4,600,000
Homes with electricity	8%	99.9%
Life expectancy (male)	46.3 years	73.6 years
Life expectancy (female)	48.3 years	79.7 years
Miles of paved road	10	4 million
Bison	400	200,000
Farms	5,740,000	2,191,510
Millionaires	3,000	3,500,000
Population	75,994,575	281,421906

Population by Ancestry

German	42,841,569	15.2%
Irish	30,524,799	10.8%
African-American	24,903,412	8.8%
English	24,509,692	8.7%
American	20,188,305	7.2%
Mexican	18,382,291	6.5%

Italian	15,63,348	5.6%
Polish	8,977,235	3.2%
French	8,309,666	3.0%
Native American	7,876,568	2.8%
Other		28%

Most Common Surnames

1   Smith

2   Johnson

3   Williams

4   Brown

5   Jones

6   Miller

7   Davis

8   Garcia

9   Rodriguez

10   Wilson

11   Martinez

Ten Most Popular Boys' Names

1 Jacob

2 Michael

3 Ethan

4 Joshua

5 Daniel

6 Christopher

7 Anthony

8 William

9 Matthew

10 Andrew

Ten Most Popular Girls' Names

1 Emily

2 Isabella

3 Emma

4 Ava

5 Madison

6 Sophia

7 Olivia

8 Abigail

9 Hannah

10 Elizabeth

Seniors

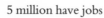 Approximately 38 million Americans are over 65

 9.1 million are military veterans

 5 million have jobs

50,000 are enrolled in college

 56% are married

31% are widowed

★ 81% own their own homes

★ 78% own their own vehicle

★ 40% have a computer in their home

★ The densest population of seniors is in Florida (17%)

Family and Society

Approximately:

 76.2 million family units;

 73 million children under the age of 18;

 3.8 million children live with their grandparents;

★ 17.6 million college students;

★ 9% of the population partake in some form of educational activity;

 99% of the population aged 15 and over is literate;

 153.1 million people in the labor force;

★ 12% of the population live below the poverty line;

83% of women spend some time doing household activities on an average day, compared to 66% of men;

 255 million cell phones;

21% of men participate in sports or exercise (16% of women).

Women by Numbers

Total female population	152 million
Mothers	82.5 million
Stay-at-home mothers	5.6 million
Average number of children per adult woman	1.9
Median annual earnings of women over 16 (permanent, full-time workers)	$32,168
Women over 25 who have completed high school	85.4%
Women over 25 with a bachelor's degree	26.1 million
Women who voted in the 2004 presidential election	65%
Proportion of the armed forces who are female	15%
Female military veterans	1.7 million

Ten Largest Native American Tribes

1 Cherokee: 729,533

2 Navajo: 298,197

3 Latin American: 180,774

4 Choctaw: 158,774

5 Sioux: 153,360

6 Chippewa: 149,669

7 Apache: 96,833

8 Blackfeet: 85,750

9 Iroquois: 80,822

10 Pueblo: 74,085

Winners of the Nobel Prize for Literature

 Sinclair Lewis, 1930

Eugene O'Neill, 1936

★ Pearl S Buck, 1938

★ William Faulkner, 1949

★ Ernest Hemingway, 1954

★ John Steinbeck, 1962

★ Saul Bellow, 1976

★ Isaac Bashevis Singer, 1978

★ Czeslaw Milosz, 1980

★ Toni Morrison, 1993

Mark Twain Quotes

"Be careful about reading health books. You may die of a misprint."

"Don't go around saying the world owes you a living. The world owes you nothing. It was here first."

"I have never let my schooling interfere with my education."

"The man who doesn't read good books has no advantage over the man who can't read them."

"Why do you sit there looking like an envelope without an address on it?"

Food

★ Americans spend approximately $1 billion a day on eating out and approximately $25 billion a year on beer.

★ Americans consumed over 3.1 billion pounds of chocolate in 2001.

★ The first American restaurant to use printed menus was Delmonico's Steak House in New York in 1837.

★ NASA has included hot dogs on the menu on space flights.

★ The first credit card was issued in 1951, when the Diner's Club issued cards that people could use in selected restaurants in New York City.

★ Sliced bread and fortune cookies were both invented in America.

★ Pizza Hut is the largest pizza franchise in the world.

★ About 25% of American commuters eat breakfast on their way to work.

★ The average American spends $20,000 on fast food in their lifetime.

The first McDonalds restaurant opened in 1948 in San Bernardino, California.

 The first Burger King restaurant opened in 1954 in Miami, Florida.

Success

"Flaming enthusiasm, backed by horse sense and persistence, is the quality that most frequently makes for success."

Dale Carnegie

"You only have to do a very few things right in your life so long as you don't do too many things wrong."

Warren Buffet

"A person is a success if he gets up in the morning and gets to bed at night and in between does what he wants to do."

Bob Dylan

"Actually, I'm an overnight success. But it took 20 years."

Monty Hall

"I don't measure a man's success by how high he climbs but how high he bounces when he hits bottom."

General George S Patton

"Eighty percent of success is showing up."

Woody Allen

"I don't know the key to success, but the key to failure is trying to please everybody."

Bill Cosby

"You will find the key to success under the alarm clock."

Benjamin Franklin

"It is wise to keep in mind that neither success nor failure is ever final."

Roger Babson

4

HISTORY

Brief History

Some time before 12,000 BCE	North American native people inhabit the land
1000	Norse seaman Leif Ericsson sets foot on North America. Lands in Newfoundland; names it Vinland
1492	Christopher Columbus arrives in the Americas – landing on the island now known as San Salvador, in the Bahamas (first of four voyages)
1513	Spanish explorer, Juan Ponce de Leon, arrives on the coast of Florida
1565	Saint Augustine, Florida, becomes the first permanent European

colony in North America (settled by the Spanish)

1607	Jamestown, Virginia, becomes the first permanent English settlement in America
1619	First African slaves brought to mainland North America
1650	Colonial population reaches 50,000
1664	English take over New Amsterdam from the Dutch; rename it New York
1754–1763	British begin to gain control over eastern North America in the French and Indian War (Treaty of Paris signed 1763)
1773	Boston Tea Party: Colonial patriots (disguised as Native Americans) board three ships in Boston Harbor and throw hundreds of crates of tea overboard as a protest against the British tea tax
1774	First Continental Congress meets in Philadelphia
1775	American Revolution – War of Independence fought between Britain and the 13 British colonies on the east coast
1776	In Philadelphia, Continental Congress adopts the Declaration of Independence (July 4)

1789	George Washington unanimously elected President of the United States
1800	Washington DC becomes federal capital (replacing Philadelphia)
1803	Louisiana Purchase: US pays just over $11 million dollars for 828,800 square miles of former French territory encompassing the Mississippi Valley
1812	US declares war on Britain, due to confrontation over shipping
1819	Florida becomes part of the United States (previously under Spanish control)
1830	President Jackson signs the Indian Removal Act, approving the removal of Native American tribes from the east
1836	Texas declares independence from Mexico
1846	US declares war on Mexico in an effort to take California and other territory in the southwest
1861	Civil War starts between North and South over the issue of slavery expanding into the western states
1863	Homestead Act, allowing settlers to claim ownership of land they've

	lived on for more than five years, becomes law
1867	Alaska purchased from Russia for $7.2 million
1876	Battle of Little Big Horn. Lt Col George Custer's regiment wiped out by Sioux tribe under the famous Native American chief Sitting Bull in Montana
1886	Statue of Liberty is given to America by France to celebrate the Centennial of the signing of the Declaration of Independence
1898	USS Maine blown up in Havana harbor, leading to start of Spanish–American War
1898	US annexes Hawaii by Act of Congress
1899	US acquires American Samoa by treaty
1903	US acquires Panama Canal Zone
1917	US declares war on Germany and Austro-Hungarian Empire (World War I)
1920	Women win the right to vote (19th Amendment of the constitution)
1929	Stock market crash kicks off the Great Depression
1941	Japan attacks Pearl Harbor; US enters World War II

1950	Korean War begins
1963	President John F Kennedy assassinated
1969	Neil Armstrong and Edwin (Buzz) Aldrin become the first people to walk on the Moon
1974	President Nixon resigns following Watergate scandal
1991	Operation Desert Storm: US and its allies drive Iraqis out of Kuwait
2001	9/11: Terrorist attacks by airplane on World Trade Center (New York), Pentagon (Washington); fourth plane crashes in Philadelphia
2008	Wall Street and American financial institutions suffer their worst losses in decades

Inventions, Firsts, and Beginnings

1787 First steamboats unveiled, one on the Delaware River and one on the Potomac River

1790 Start of industrial era in the US as first water-powered cotton mill begins operation in Rhode Island

1792 US Mint opens

1795	First official US military weapon – the Springfield musket – begins manufacture
1801	First iron suspension bridge in US is built – Jacob's Creek, Westmoreland, Pennsylvania
1825	Great Lakes and Hudson River linked by the Erie Canal
1827	First (12-seat) horse-drawn bus service (in New York)
1831	Electric motor invented by Joseph Henry
1836	The Colt Six-Shooter engineered by Samuel Colt
1838	First Morse telegraph message ("A patient waiter is no loser") sent in US, in New Jersey
1844	First express delivery service started by Henry Wells; later developed into the Wells Fargo Company
1894	First telephone switchboard – Boston, Massachusetts
1879	The first milk bottles used by a dairy in Brooklyn, New York
1883	Brooklyn Bridge opens to pedestrian traffic
1885	First skyscraper built in Chicago with 10 storeys
1889	First pay telephone installed in a bank in Hartford, Connecticut
1894	Oil discovered in Texas
1896	Henry Ford builds first motor vehicle (the Quadricycle)

1897   US Navy launches USS Holland – its first submarine with an internal combustion engine and electric motor

1903   William Harley and Arthur and Walter Davidson found the Harley-Davidson motorcycle company

1911   Chevrolet Motor Company starts trading

1919   Pop-up toaster invented by Charles Strite (patented 1921)

1926   David Sarnoff founds the National Broadcasting Company (NBC)

1927   Transatlantic telephone service begins between New York and London

1935   Alcoholics Anonymous (AA) founded in Akron, Ohio

1935   US Army begins operating B-17 bombers – one of the most important military aircraft ever built

1939   First commercial transatlantic passenger airline service starts (between New York and France)

1943   The Pentagon, the world's largest office building, is completed, at a cost of $83 million

1943   First full-scale plutonium production reactor begins operation in Hanford, Washington

1945   First atomic bomb tested at Alamogordo, New Mexico

1948   Albert the monkey launched into space in the nose cone of a V-2 rocket

1958	US launches its first artificial satellite – Explorer I
1961	Alan B Shephard Jr. is first American in space
1969	Neil Armstrong is first man to walk on the Moon
1975	Bill Gates and Paul Allen found Microsoft
1976	Stephen Wozniak and Steve Jobs design the first Apple computer

The Great Depression

 The stock market crash of 1929 resulted in stockholders losing $40 billion. It came during a time when the value of real estate was declining and investor confidence was at an all-time low.

 Over 9,000 banks failed during the 1930s. Bank deposits were uninsured and people simply lost their savings.

 Individuals from all walks of life became very cautious in their spending because of the economic uncertainty. This decreased demand for goods led to a fall in production, which led to a reduction in the workforce, which led to reduced wages and spending.

 In 1930, the government created an import tariff (the Smoot-Hawley Act) to protect American companies. This led to less trade with foreign companies as well as economic retaliation.

Many farms and related businesses failed as a result of a severe drought in the Mississippi Valley in 1930.

 In the 1930s, food riots began across the country; grocery shops were regularly looted.

 In April 1930, more than 750,000 New Yorkers were listed as reliant on city relief.

 America only began to come out of the Depression when it entered World War II, which kick-started US industry.

War and Peace

Formal declarations of war by Congress and their date of conclusion by treaty:

War of 1812 (against the British Empire)
>June 18, 1812 to December 24, 1814

Mexican–American War
>May 11, 1846 to February 2, 1848

Spanish–American War
>April 24, 1898 to December 10, 1898

World War I
>against Germany, April 6, 1917
>against Austro-Hungarian Empire, December 7, 1917 to June 4, 1920

World War II

> against Japan, December 8, 1941 to September 8, 1951
>
> against Germany and Italy, December 11, 1941 to May 8, 1945
>
> against Bulgaria, Hungary, and Romania, June 5, 1942 to February 10, 1947

Military Engagements Authorized by Congress

Twelve instances of military engagements authorized by Congress fell short of formal declarations of war:

★ 1798: Quasi-War against France

★ 1801: First Barbary War

★ 1815: Second Barbary War

★ 1820: Raid on slave traffickers in Africa

★ 1859: Redress for attack on US Navy vessel by Paraguay

★ 1918: Intervention during the Russian Civil War

★ 1958: Lebanon crisis

★ 1964: Vietnam War

★ 1983: Intervention against Shi'a and Druze militia in Lebanon and Syria

1991: First Gulf War (Operation Desert Storm)

1. 2001: War in Afghanistan (Operation Enduring Freedom)

2003: Iraq War (Operation Iraqi Freedom)

Failed Constitutional Amendments

1893   To rename the US the "United States of the Earth"

1893   To abolish the United States Army and Navy

1914   To make divorce illegal

1916   To put all acts of war to the vote

1933   To limit personal wealth to $1 million

1971   To give Americans the right to a pollution-free environment

Independence Day – July 4

 Commemorates the formal adoption of the Declaration of Independence in 1776

Declared a legal holiday in 1941

 Liberty Bell rung on July 8, 1776 to announce the Declaration of Independence

Marked by George Washington in 1778 by the issue of a double ration of rum to the soldiery

 Chance that hot dogs and pork sausages eaten on Independence Day come from Iowa – 1 in 4

 Value of fireworks imported annually from China (majority used at Independence Day celebrations) – $206.3 million

Civil War Firsts

 Black field officer – Martin Delaney

 "General of the Army" – Ulysses S Grant

Military attack on an oil installation (Burning Springs, Virginia)

"Dog tags" used for military identification (paper or material pinned to the soldiers' uniforms)

Battle between ironclad vessels (Hampton Roads, Virginia, March 1862)

Vice-president volunteering for military service (Hannibal Hamlin)

 Awarding of medals to black soldiers (Butler Medal)

American female civilian killed in a major battle (Judith Henry, 1861)

Declaration of allegiance to the Confederacy by a Native American tribe (Choctaw 1861)

 Sinking of a ship by a submarine vessel (USS Housatonic by CSS H.L. Hunley, Charleston Harbor, 1864)

 Black troops fighting on the Union side (Battle of Port Hudson, Louisiana 1863)

 Canned rations given to troops

 Congressional Medal of Honor awarded twice to the same person (Lieutenant Thomas Custer)

 Gatling machine gun used in battle

Legislation allowing the United States to draft men into military service (National Conscription Act 1863)

Civil War Mascots

 General Lee's hen, which handily also provided eggs for his breakfast

 "Jack," a bull terrier, 102 Pennsylvania Infantry

 "Old Abe," an eagle, 8 Wisconsin

 "Old Harvey," a white bulldog, 104 Ohio

"York," a setter, pet of Brig. Gen. Alexander S Asboth

 "Sallie," a Staffordshire Bull Terrier, 11 Pennsylvania; depicted on the unit's monument at Gettysburg

Nicknames of Civil War Generals

Spoons	Major General Benjamin Butler – allegedly for stealing the silver cutlery while on occupation duty in New Orleans.
Stonewall	Lieutenant General Thomas A Jackson – for his ability to stay calm in battle.
Old Wooden Head	Major General Henry Halleck – reputedly not the brightest-ever commander.
Old Stars	Major General Ormsby MacKnight Mitchell – had previously been an astronomer.
Grumble	Brigadier General E Jones – complained about everything.
Kill Cavalry	Major General Judson Kilpatrick – tended to put his men into dangerous situations.
Bullhead	Major General Edwin Vose Sumner

	– a musket ball allegedly bounced off his head.
Neighbor	Major General David Jones – for his friendly personality.
Little Phil	Major General Philip Sheridan – for his short stature.
Forty-eight Hours	Major General Abner Doubleday – was slow and unenthusiastic about making decisions.
Tardy George	Major General George Sykes – very slow at command decisions.
Pathfinder	Major General John C Fremont – for his reputation as an explorer.
Old Slow Trot	Major General George Thomas – for his slow but steady style of leadership.

Popular Songs of the Civil War

★ "Dixie" (Dan Emmet)

★ "Maryland, My Maryland" (James Ryder Randall)

★ "The Bonnie Blue Flag" (Henry MacCarthy)

★ "When This Cruel War is Over" (Charlie C Sawyer)

★ "Tenting on the Old Camp Ground" (Walter Kittredge)

★ "Lorena" (HDL Webster)

★ "All Quiet Along the Potomac Tonight" (Ethel Lynn Beers)

★ "Marching Along" (William Bradbury)

★ "Marching Through Georgia" (Henry Clay Work)

★ "Just Before the Battle, Mother" (George F Root)

★ "The Battle Cry of Freedom" (George F Root)

★ "The Battle Hymn of the Republic" (Julia Ward Howe)

★ "We are Coming Father Abraham" (James S Gibbons)

★ "Tramp, Tramp, Tramp" (George F Root)

★ "John Brown's Body" (Unknown)

Civil War Generals' Civilian Occupations

★ George Beale, Bookbinder

★ Elon Farnsworth, Wagonmaster

★ Edward Ferrero, Dancing Master

★ Benjamin Grierson, Music Teacher

★ Charles Heckman, Railroad Conductor

★ Mark Lowery, Bricklayer

★ George McGinnis, Hatter

★ John McNeil, Hatter

★ Ormsby MacKnight Mitchell, Astronomer

★ Erastus Tyler, Furrier

Commemorative Stamps

		(millions saved)
1992	Wildflowers	76.1
1993	Elvis	124.1
1993	Rock and Roll/Rhythm and Blues	75.9
1999	Insects and Spiders	61.0
2000	Legends of Baseball	53.9
2002	Greetings from America	71.4
2006	Art of Disney Romance	57.2
2006	DC Comics Superheroes	73.0
2006	Wonders of America	87.5

5

TOURISM

Ten Fascinating Facts

1 50.9 million international travelers visited the United States in 2000.

2 In 2006, international travelers spent $22.2 billion with American airlines.

3 Tourism provides 18 million jobs (7.7 million directly employed, 10.3 million indirectly employed).

4 Travel and tourism generates $1.6 trillion annually.

5 Local, state, and federal governments gather $110 billion in tax revenue from travel and tourism.

6   Gambling accounts for more than 8% of US travel; more than 56 million people visited a casino in 2006.

7   10% of traveling involves getting to the beach.

8   Visits to theme and amusement parks count for 9% of non-business trips.

9   Business travel accounts for 18% of trips.

10   Approximately 42 million Americans travel at least once a year to attend a wedding, go on honeymoon, or celebrate an anniversary.

The Hotel Industry

 2.6 million hotel rooms let every day

 49,899 hotels, motels, and bed and breakfast-properties

 4.6 million hotel rooms, producing $154 billion annually

 Average occupancy rate – 63%

 Average room rate – $100 per night (January 2009)

 Average stay – 3.2 nights

 41% of travelers travel alone (71% of business travelers)

Conrad Hilton purchased his first hotel, The Mobley, in Cisco, Texas in 1919

 Western Hotels chain, now Westin, started in the Pacific Northwest in 1929

 Sheraton was the first hotel corporation to be listed on the New York Stock Exchange, in 1945

First Holiday Inn opened in Memphis, Tennessee in 1952

World Heritage Sites

Cahokia Mounds State Historic Site, Illinois:
> Former centre of the Mississippian Native American Culture, has the largest prehistoric earth constructions in the Americas

Carlsbad Caverns National Park, New Mexico:
> Network of over 80 caves; contains the country's deepest cave (1,597 ft)

Chaco Culture National Historical Park, New Mexico:
> Large multi-level stone villages built by the Anasazi tribe, includes 400-mile road system in the Chaco Canyon

Everglades National Park, Florida:
> "River of grass:" body of water 6 inches deep and 50 miles wide; flows south-west at about ¼ mile a day

Glacier Bay National Park and Preserve, Alaska:
>Nine tidewater glaciers; has no roads

Grand Canyon National Park, Arizona:
>Geological wonder, created over 6 million years by the Colorado River; 1 mile deep, 277 miles long; up to 18 miles wide

Great Smoky Mountains National Park, North Carolina/Tennessee:
>Named the "Place of Blue Smoke" by the Cherokee tribe; forest exudes water vapor and oily residue to create a smoke-like haze

Hawaii Volcanoes National Park, Hawaii:
>Contains the world's most massive volcano, Mauna Loa, 13,677 ft

Independence Hall, Philadelphia, Pennsylvania:
>Declaration of Independence and the Constitution both signed here

Mammoth Cave National Park, Kentucky:
>Estimated to have between 340 and 365 miles of passages

Mesa Verde National Park, Colorado:
>Series of multi-level buildings built by the Anasazi tribe

Monticello/University of Virginia, Charlottesville, Virginia:
>Estate belonging to Thomas Jefferson, principal author of the Declaration of Independence and

third US president; founder of University of Virginia

Olympic National Park, Washington:
Mount Olympus (7,965 ft), glaciers, temperate rainforests

Redwood National Park, California:
Home to the tallest trees in the world, the California redwood, which can grow up to 350 feet over 400 years; some over 2,000 years old

Taos Pueblo, New Mexico:
Communal housing constructed by the Taos Pueblo tribe in the fourteenth century

Waterton–Glacier International Peace Park, Montana:
World's first international peace park; spans two countries (US and Canada)

Wrangell–St Elias National Park and Preserve, Alaska:
Over 2,000 glaciers and ice fields

Yosemite National Park, California:
Spectacular granite cliffs and waterfalls; 3.2 million visitors in 2006

Yellowstone National Park:
First national park in the US; contains half of the world's geothermal features, such as the "Old Faithful" geyser

Top Ten City Destinations

By visitor numbers

★ New York City: 7.7 million

★ Los Angeles: 2.7 million

★ Miami: 2.3 million

★ San Francisco: 2.3 million

★ Orlando: 2.1 million

★ Las Vegas: 1.7 million

★ Honolulu: 1.6 million

★ Washington DC: 1.2 million

★ Chicago: 1.1 million

★ Boston: 1 million

Most Visited States

★ New York: 7.9 million

★ California: 5.18 million

★ Florida: 4.68 million

★ Hawaii: 1.86 million

★ Nevada: 1.77 million

★ Massachusetts: 1.17 million

★ Illinois: 1.17 million

★ Texas: 1.00 million

★ New Jersey: 0.721 million

Disneyland

★ Near Anaheim, California

★ Opened July 17, 1955

★ More than 520 million visitors

★ Cost $16 million to build

★ Covers 160 acres, of which 85 acres are open to the public

★ Has 8 themed lands: Main Street USA, Adventureland, New Orleans Square, Frontierland, Critter Country, Fantasyland, Mickey's Toontown, and Tomorrowland

★ Sleeping Beauty's Castle is covered in gold leaf so it glitters even on cloudy days

★ Lost and Found Department collects more than 400 items a day

★ Visitors produce 30 tons of rubbish a day

★ Sells more than 4 million burgers a year

★ King Arthur's Carousel has 68 horses, no two of which are the same

★ Three unscheduled closures since 1955: 1963, due to President Kennedy's assassination; 1970, due to demonstrations against the Vietnam war; 2001, due to the terrorist attacks on September 11

Weird Tourist Attractions

Atomic Bomb Crater (Mars Bluff, South Carolina):
   Created after an (unarmed) atomic bomb was accidentally dropped on a farm in 1958; 75 ft wide

The Five-Storey-Tall Chicken (Marietta, Georgia):
   A huge sheet-metal statue of a chicken, over 50 ft high

Hobbiton USA (Phillipsville, California):
   Life-sized Hobbit village, based on *The Lord of the Rings*

Holy Land USA (Waterbury, Connecticut):
   Model of the Holy Land, now in decay

Philip Morris Cigarette Tours (Richmond, Virginia):
>Factory tours showing how cigarettes are made

Soup Tureen Museum (Camden, New Jersey):
>Charting the Campbell's soup story

Spam Museum (Austin, Minnesota):
>Dedicated to the history of Spam (not the email kind!)

Spongeorama (Tarpon Springs, Florida):
>All you ever wanted to know about sponges

Toilet Rock (City of Rocks, New Mexico):
>Giant rock formation in the shape of a toilet

World's Largest Office Chair (Anniston, Alabama):
>Over 30 ft high

World's Largest Stump (Kokomo, Indiana):
>Massive sycamore stump, 800 years old; 57 ft in diameter; 12 ft high

The Statue of Liberty

★ Formal name is "Liberty Enlightening the World"

★ Construction began in Paris, France in 1875; completed in June 1884

★ Gift to the American people from the people of France to celebrate the friendship established between the two countries during the American Revolution

Reassembled in the United States, October 1886

 Unveiled by President Grover Cleveland, despite the fact that as Governor of New York he had vetoed a bill to contribute $50,000 to the building of the pedestal

 The crown has 25 windows and seven spikes symbolizing the seven seas and continents

 Inscription on the tablet reads: July IV MDC-CLXXVI (July 4, 1776)

 Visited by more than four million people a year

 150 ft tall from base to torch; 305 ft tall from ground to tip of torch

 Hand 16 ft 5 in long; index finger 8 ft; fingernails 13 in by 10 in

 Eyes 2 ft 6 in across; 35-ft waistline

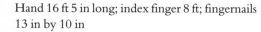 Functioned as a lighthouse from 1886 to 1902; could be seen up to 24 miles away

Ellis Island

 Named after Samuel Ellis who owned it in the 1770s

★ Called "Kioshk" (Gull Island) by Native Americans; known as Oyster Island by the early colonists

★ More than 12 million migrants entered the Unites States through the portal of Ellis Island between 1892 and 1954; approximately 1.25 million immigrants were processed in 1907 alone

★ Approximately 2% of immigrants were refused entry

★ First immigrant to be officially processed through Ellis Island was a 15-year-old Irish girl, Annie Moore, on January 1, 1892

★ The immigration centre burned down on June 14, 1897

★ During World War II, enemy merchant seamen were detained in the baggage and dormitory building

★ Immediately after World War II, the island was a Coast Guard training base and internment camp for enemy aliens

★ Some 7,000 aliens were interned on the island; in November 1954, the last detainee, a Norwegian seaman, Arne Peterssen, was released and Ellis Island officially closed

The Ellis Island Immigration Museum receives almost two million visitors a year

Best Beaches

Source: *America's Best Beaches* by Dr. Stephen P Leatherman (aka Dr. Beach, Professor of Environmental Studies at Florida International University)

1 Caladesi Island State Park, Dunedin, Florida

2 Hanalei Bay, Kauai, Hawaii

3 Siesta Beach, Sarasota, Florida

4 Coopers Beach, Southampton, New York

5 Coronado Beach, San Diego, California

6 Main Beach, East Hampton, New York

7 Hamoa Beach, Maui, Hawaii

8 Cape Hatteras, Outer Banks, North Carolina

9 Cape Florida State Park, Key Biscayne, Florida

10 Beachwalker Park, Kiawah Island, South Carolina

Federal Holidays

January 1	New Year's Day
Third Monday in January	Martin Luther King, Jr Day

Third Monday in February	President's Day
Last Monday in May	Memorial Day
July 4	Independence Day
First Monday in September	Labor Day
Second Monday in October	Columbus Day
11 November	Veterans Day
Fourth Thursday in November	Thanksgiving
25 December	Christmas Day

Important National Days

February 2: Groundhog Day
    Signifies the end of winter

First Sunday of February: Super Bowl Sunday
    Final of the National Football League
    playoffs

Mardi Gras
    "Fat Tuesday;" last day before start of Lent

March 17: St Patrick's Day
    Celebrates Irish heritage and culture

April 22: Earth Day
    Promotes the protection of the environment

May 5: Cinco de Mayo
    Celebrates Mexican Independence Day

June 14: Flag Day
> Honors the American flag

Election Day
> First Tuesday after the first Monday in November (every four years)

Black Friday
> First Friday after the fourth Friday in November: marks the beginning of the Christmas shopping period

December 7: Pearl Harbor Day
> Commemorates the Japanese attack on Pearl Harbor in 1941

6

SPORTS

Ten Fascinating Facts

1   Baseball's rules were invented in 1845 by Alexander Cartwright of the Knickerbocker Baseball club.

2   A baseball home plate is 17 inches wide.

3   Soldier Field is the oldest stadium in the NFL.

4   The Los Angeles Rams were the first professional football team to have an insignia on their helmets (yellow horns).

5   Jesse Owens broke 5 world records and equaled a 6th in 45 minutes in 1935.

6   In baseball, a forfeited game is 9–0.

7   In 1972, the Dallas Cowboys were the first NFL team to hire a professional cheerleading squad.

8   In 1970, only 127 people ran the New York Marathon (now more than 40,000).

9   A regulation football field is 360 feet long and 160 feet wide.

10   "Nike" was formally known as "Blue Ribbon Sports."

National Football League Records

 Most career rushing yards: Emmit Smith, 18,355 yards (1990–2004)

 Most consecutive games won: New England Patriots, 19 (2006–2007)

 Longest streak of throwing at least one touchdown pass per game: Johnny Unitas, 47 games (1956–1960)

 Most career receiving yards: Jerry Rice, 22,895 yards (1985–2004)

 Most seasons leading the NFL in rushing yards: Jim Brown, 8 (1957–1961, 1963–1965)

 Most interceptions in a season: Dick "Night Train" Lane, 14 (1952)

 Most consecutive games played by a non-kicker: Jim Marshall, 282 (1960–1979)

 Most sacks in a single game: Derrick Thomas, 7 (1990)

Most touchdown passes thrown in a season: Tom Brady, 50 (2007)

National Basketball Association Records

 Best regular-season team winning percentage: Chicago Bulls, 72–10, 87.8% (1995–1996)

 Most regular season games played: Robert Parish, 1,611 (1976–1997)

 Most points in a single game: Wilt Chamberlain, 100 (1962)

 Most NBA championships as a player: Bill Russell, 11

Most career 3-point field goals: Reggie Miller, 2,560 (1987–2005)

 Most seasons leading the league in scoring: Michael Jordan, 10

Highest scoring average, single season: Wilt Chamberlain, 50.4 (1961–1962)

Most career assists: John Stockton, 15,806

Most rebounds in a single game: Wilt Chamberlain, 55 (1960)

 Most career points scored: Kareem Abdul-Jabbar, 38,387 (1969–1989)

Major League Baseball Records

 Most career wins: Cy Young, 511 (1890–1911)

 Most career strikeouts: Nolan Ryan, 5,714

 Most career hits: Pete Rose, 4,256 (1963–1986)

 Most career stolen bases: Rickey Henderson, 1,406 (1979–2003)

 Most runs batted in (season): Lewis Robert "Hack" Wilson, 191 (1930)

 Longest hitting streak: Joe Di Maggio, 56 games (1941)

 Highest season batting average (modern era, post 1901): Nap Lajoie, .426 (1901)

 Most career shutouts: Walter Johnson, 110 (1907–1927)

 Most consecutive games played: Cal Ripken, 2,632 (1982–1998)

Record Holders

Rocky Marciano	Undefeated streak, retiring as heavyweight champ, 49–0

Lance Armstrong	Seven consecutive *Tour de France* wins (1999–2005)
Oklahoma Sooners	Forty-seven consecutive NCAA Division 1–A football victories
UCLA Bruins	Seven consecutive NCAA basketball titles (1967–1973)
Wayne Gretzky	2,857 NHL career points (1979–1999)
Richard Petty	Twenty-seven NASCAR race wins in one season (1967)
University of North Carolina Women's Soccer team	103 consecutive games without a loss (1986–1990)

Sporting Firsts

 Steve Fosset: first man to circumnavigate the world in a balloon, 2002 (his sixth attempt)

 Eddie Matthews of the Milwaukee Braves: first person to appear on the front cover of *Sports Illustrated*, 1954

 Max McGee of the Green Bay Packers: first person to score a Super Bowl touchdown, 1967

 New York Yankees: first World Series win, 1923

Bob Pettit: first NBA player to score 20,000 points, 1964

 Citation: first horse to reach $1 million in career earnings

 Cap Anson: first baseball player to reach 3,000 career hits, 1897

 Georges Carpentier v Jack Dempsey: first million-dollar gate for a boxing match, 1921

 Billie Jean King: first sportswoman to be named Athlete of the Year by *Sports Illustrated*, 1972

Tidiest Sports Stats

 Joe Gordon: 1,000 hits in 1,000 games with the New York Yankees

 Richard Petty: won his 200th NASCAR race in Daytona Beach on July 4, 1976 (his last win)

 Elvin Hayes: played exactly 50,000 minutes in his NBA basketball career

 Lefty Grove, baseball player and Hall of Famer: won exactly 300 games during his career

 Enos Slaughter: career batting average of .300

Roberto Clemente of the Pittsburgh Pirates: exactly 3,000 hits in his playing career (cut short by a plane crash)

Northern Dancer: ran the Kentucky Derby in precisely 2:00:00 in 1964

Gregg Pruitt (Cleveland Browns 1976), Willie Ellison (Los Angeles Rams 1971), and Mercury Morris (Miami Dolphins 1972): rushed for exactly 1,000 yards in a season

Memorable Sporting Uniform Numbers

100   During his sophomore and junior years, place-kicker Bill Bell scored exactly 100 points wearing number 12. He went on to wear number 100 for the University of Kansas.

96   Bill Voiselle, major-league pitcher, was from the town of Ninety-Six, South Carolina.

85   Petr Kilma, NHL forward, wore number 85 to celebrate the year he defected from Czechoslovakia.

50   Sid Fernandez, New York Mets pitcher, wore number 50 to honor his native Hawaii, 50th state in the union.

7   John Neves, minor league baseball player, wore a backwards 7 on his shirt (check his second name!).

Olympic Host Cities

1904	Summer Olympics	St Louis, Missouri
1932	Winter Olympics	Lake Placid, New York
1932	Summer Olympics	Los Angeles, California
1960	Winter Olympics	Squaw Valley, California
1980	Winter Olympics	Lake Placid, New York
1984	Summer Olympics	Los Angeles, California
1996	Summer Olympics	Atlanta, Georgia
2002	Winter Olympics	Salt Lake City, Utah

The Olympics

 More medals (2,189) at the Summer Olympics than any other country

 Hosted the Olympic Games eight times

 Thirty-six gold medals at both the 2008 Beijing Summer Olympics and the 2004 Athens Summer Olympics

 Michael Phelps won a record eight gold medals for swimming in the Beijing Olympics – would have been joint ninth if he'd been a country

Famous Sporting Quotes

"Float like a butterfly, sting like a bee."
Muhammad Ali on how to defeat
Sonny Liston in their 1964 fight

"It ain't over 'till the fat lady sings."

> Coach Dick Motta of the Washington
> Bullets, optimistic despite his team trailing
> 2 games to 1 in the 1978 NBA finals; he
> was right – Washington won the series
> in seven games

"Thanks, King."

> Jim Thorpe's (alleged) response to King
> Gustav V of Sweden, after the King presented
> a bust of himself to Thorpe after he won the
> 1912 Stockholm Olympic pentathlon

"You are the pits of the world."

> John McEnroe to the Wimbledon umpire
> in his first round match against
> Tom Gullikson in 1981

"Nice guys finish last."

> Leo Durocher, manager of the Brooklyn
> Dodgers, talking to the press before a game
> with the last-placed New York Giants

"Say it ain't so, Joe."

> Plea allegedly made by a small boy outside
> the court after Joe Jackson testified in the grand
> jury investigation of the 1919 Chicago Black Sox

"We wuz robbed."

> Joe Jacobs, after his fighter Max Schmeling lost
> the heavyweight championship to Jack Sharkey
> in a 15th round decision (New York, June 1932)

"He can run but he can't hide."

> Joe Louis before his heavyweight
> title fight against Billy Conn

Football Quotes

"The spirit, the will to win, and the will to excel are the things that endure. These qualities are so much more than the events that occur."

Vince Lombardi, legendary football coach

"I want to rush for 1,000 or 1,500 yards, whichever comes first."

George Rogers, running back

"For me, winning isn't something that happens suddenly on the field when the whistle blows and the crowds roar. Winning is something that builds physically and mentally every day that you train and every night that you dream."

Emmitt Smith, running back

"If my mother put on a helmet and shoulder pads and a uniform that wasn't the same as the one I was wearing, I'd run over her if she was in my way. And I love my mother."

Bo Jackson, running back

"I'm the football coach around here and don't you remember it."

Bill Petterson, football coach

"Men, I want you just thinking of one word all season. One word and one word only: Super Bowl."

Bill Petterson, football coach

"It's a humbling thing being humble."

Former Ohio State running back Maurice Clarett, referring to the 2005 draft

"The shoulder surgery was a success. The lobotomy failed."

Mike Ditka, on quarterback Jim McMahon's surgery

"He treats us like men. He lets us wear earrings."

Torrin Polk, on his coach John Jenkins

Baseball Quotes

"There's a deep fly ball. Winfield goes back, back … his head hits the wall … its rolling towards second base."

Jerry Coleman, commentator

"If horses can't eat it, I won't play on it."

Dick Allen, Major League Baseball player

"Why does everybody stand up and sing 'Take me out to the ballgame' when they're already there?"

Larry Anderson, Major League Baseball pitcher

"Baseball is 90% mental – the other half is physical."

Peter "Yogi" Berra, Major League Baseball player

"They shouldn't throw at me. I'm the father of five or six kids."

Baseball player Tito Fuentes, after being hit by a pitch

"I'm not an athlete. I'm a professional baseball player."

John Kruk, Major League Baseball player

"Like they say, it ain't over 'till the fat guy swings."

Philadelphia Phillies catcher Darren Daulton, on stocky baseman John Kruk

"The game was closer than the score indicated."

Baseball player Dizzy Dean, after a 1–0 game

"Therapy can be a good thing: It can be therapeutic."

Yankee's Alan Rodriguez, on the benefits of seeing a therapist

"It took me seventeen years to get three thousand hits in baseball. I did it in one afternoon on the golf course."

Hank Aaron, baseball player

Basketball Quotes

"I've missed more than 9,000 shots in my career. I've lost almost 300 games. Twenty-six times, I've been trusted to take the game-winning shot and I've missed. I've failed over and over again in my life. And that is why I succeed."

Michael Jordan, NBA basketball player

"Left hand, right hand: It doesn't matter. I'm amphibious."

Charles Shackleford, NBA basketball player

"We're going to turn this team around 360 degrees."

Jason Kidd, NBA basketball player

"Talent wins games, but teamwork and intelligence win championships."

Michael Jordan, NBA basketball player

"Because there are no fours."

NBA player Antoine Walker, asked why he shot so many threes

"My sister's expecting a baby, and I don't know if I'm going to be an uncle or an aunt."

Chuck Nevitt, North Carolina State basketball player

"I've won at every level, except college and pro."

Shaquille O'Neal, on his lack of championship wins

"Tom."

Tom Nissalke, coach of the NBA's Houston Rockets, asked how to pronounce his name

7

MUSIC

Brief History

1640   The *Bay Psalm Book*, first book printed in British Colonial America (in Cambridge, MA), contains religious music

c. 1775   British soldiers sing *Yankee Doodle* as a way of making fun of the colonists; backfires when the Americans adopt it as their anthem

1814   Francis Scott Key writes *The Star-Spangled Banner*, set to the tune of an old British drinking song *To Anacreon in Heaven*

1842   Philharmonic Society of New York founded

1878   New York Symphony Orchestra founded

1881   Boston Symphony Orchestra founded

1883   Metropolitan Opera House established in New York

1891	Carnegie Hall opens in New York
c. 1900	"Country" music becomes popular in the southeast; originates from Irish, Scottish, and English folk songs and ballads; features stringed instruments, such as the guitar, banjo, and fiddle, and the harmonica
c. 1900	"Western" music takes hold in the western States; features steel guitars and large bands
c. 1900	Jazz starts to develop in New Orleans (mixture of Black, French, and Spanish music)
1928	New York Symphony Orchestra merges with Philharmonic Society of New York to become the New York Philharmonic-Symphony Orchestra
1931	President Herbert Hoover and Congress confirm *The Star-Spangled Banner* as the national anthem
1948	Columbia Records introduces long-playing vinyl records
1951	"Rock 'n' roll" introduced to the public by Cleveland disc jockey Alan Freed, in an effort to promote rhythm and blues to white audiences
1955	Elvis Presley becomes famous throughout America and the world
1959	Grammy awards begin; introduced by the National Academy of Recording Arts and Sciences

1969	Woodstock Festival
1977	*Saturday Night Fever* released
1979	Sony launch the Walkman
1981	MTV launched
1981	Compact discs introduced to replace vinyl records
2000	Portable media players launched

Songs that Debuted at Number One in the Billboard Singles Chart

 Michael Jackson, *You Are Not Alone* (September 1995)

 Mariah Carey, *Fantasy* (September 1995)

 Whitney Houston, *Exhale* (November 1995)

 Mariah Carey and Boyz II Men, *One Sweet Day* (December 1995)

 Puff Daddy and Faith Evans featuring 112, *I'll Be Missing You* (June 1997)

 Mariah Carey, *Honey* (September 1997)

 Elton John, *Candle in the Wind 1997* / *Something About The Way You Look Tonight* (October 1997)

Céline Dion, *My Heart Will Go On* (February 1998)

 Aerosmith, *I Don't Want to Miss a Thing* (September 1998)

★ Lauryn Hill, *Doo Wop* (November 1998)

 R Kelly and Céline Dion, *I'm Your Angel* (December 1998)

★ Clay Aiken, *This is the Night* (June 2003)

★ Fantasia, *I Believe* (July 2004)

★ Carrie Underwood, *Inside Your Heaven* (July 2005)

★ Taylor Hicks, *Do I Make You Proud?* (July 2006)

Artists with the Most Consecutive Number One Hits

7 Whitney Houston (1985–1988)

6 The Beatles (1964–1966)

6 Bee Gees (1977–1979)

5 Elvis Presley (1959–1961)

5 The Supremes (1964–1965)

5 Michael Jackson (1987–1988)

5 Mariah Carey (1990–1991 and 1995–1998)

Best-selling Artists

1 The Beatles, 170 million

2 Garth Brooks, 128 million

3 Elvis Presley, 118.5 million

4 Led Zeppelin, 111.5 million

5 The Eagles, 100 million

6 Billy Joel, 79.5 million

7 Pink Floyd, 74.5 million

8 Barbara Streisand, 71 million

9 Elton John, 69.5 million

10 AC/DC, 69 million

Best-selling Albums

1 29 million: *The Eagles, Their Greatest Hits, 1971–1975*, The Eagles

2 27 million: *Thriller*, Michael Jackson

3 23 million: *Led Zeppelin IV*, Led Zeppelin

4 23 million: *The Wall*, Pink Floyd

5   22 million: *Back in Black*, AC/DC

6   21 million: *Greatest Hits, Volumes I & II*, Billy Joel

7   21 million: *Double Live*, Garth Brooks

8   20 million: *Come on Over*, Shania Twain

9   19 million: *The Beatles*, The Beatles

10   19 million: *Rumors*, Fleetwood Mac

Longest Broadway Runs

Phantom of the Opera	21 years	1988–Present
Cats	19 years	1982–2000
Les Miserables	17 years	1987–2003
A Chorus Line	16 years	1975–1990
Oh! Calcutta!	14 years	1976–1989
Beauty and the Beast	14 years	1994–2007
Rent	13 years	1996–Present
Chicago	13 years	1996–Present
The Lion King	12 years	1997–Present
Miss Saigon	11 years	1991–2001
42nd Street	10 years	1980–1989
Grease	9 years	1972–1980

Most Successful Concert Tours (2007)

The Police	Reunion	$212 million
Genesis	Turn it on Again	$129 million
Justin Timberlake	FutureSex/ LoveShow	$126.8 million
Kenny Chesney	Flip Flop Summer	$71.2 million
Rod Stewart	Still the Same	$70 million
Cirque Du Soleil	Delirium	$59.4 million
Roger Waters	Solo	$53.2 million
Tim McGraw & Faith Hill	Soul2Soul	$52.3 million
Christina Aguilera	Back to Basics	$48.1 million
Rascal Flatt	Me and My Gang	$41.6 million

Origins of Band Names

 The B-52s: from the popular hairstyle known as the B-52, derived from the US Air Force bomber plane.

 Beastie Boys: acronym for Boys Entering Anarchistic Stages Towards Internal Excellence.

 Counting Crows: from an old English nursery rhyme, predicting the future by counting magpies; immigrants replaced magpies with crows

The Eagles: originally known as "Teen King and the Emergencies;" decided they liked the sound of "The Eagles" which honored "The Byrds" who had heavily influenced their music.

 Eminem: real name Marshall Mathers; took his initials and phonetically rewrote.

 The Grateful Dead: originally known as "The Warlocks" but another band already had this name; Jerry Garcia found a folk tale in a book about a troubled soul put out of his misery by a traveler, hence the "grateful dead."

 Nirvana: Buddhist word; "perfect state of mind."

Skid Row: slang for a run-down neighborhood.

ZZ Top: possibly inspired by "Zig Zag" and "Top" rolling papers or possibly by famous Texas Blues man ZZ Hill.

Band Names which Feature Places

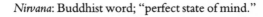 Alabama

America

Backstreet Boys (after Back Street Market in Orlando, Florida)

★ Chicago (originally Chicago Transit Authority)

★ Colorado

★ The Detroit Spinners

★ Kansas

★ Memphis

★ The New York Dolls

★ Palm Springs

Musicians Killed in Airplane Crashes

Glenn Miller, 1944	Plane crashed in the English Channel *en route* from England to France; it's unclear whether due to being shot down or caused by bad weather.
Buddy Holly, 1959	Crashed in bad weather as Holly traveled from Green Bay, Wisconsin to play a concert in Moorhead, Minnesota.
Patsy Cline, 1963	Crashed in bad weather in woodlands in Camden, Tennessee; Cline was return-

	ing from a benefit in Kansas City.
Jim Reeves, 1964	Crashed in a rainstorm traveling between Batesville, Arkansas and Nashville.
Otis Redding, 1967	Went down in Lake Monona, Madison, Wisconsin, returning from a television appearance in Cleveland, Ohio.
Jim Croce, 1973	Plane snagged the top of a tree on take-off at Natchitoches, Louisiana.
Ronnie Van Zant and Steve Gaines (Lynyrd Skynyrd), 1977	Crashed *en route* from Greenville, South Carolina to Baton Rouge, Louisiana, when their plane ran out of fuel.
Ricky Nelson, 1985	Plane caught fire and went down near De Kalb, Texas.
Aaliyah, 2001	Pilot appears to have lost control near Marsh Harbor, Bahamas; plane may have been overloaded.

Artists with Posthumous Number Ones

 Otis Redding, *Sittin' on the Dock of the Bay* (March 1968; died December 1967)

Janis Joplin, *Me and Bobby McGee* (March 1971; died October 1970)

 Jim Croce, *Time in a Bottle* (December 1973; died September 1973)

 John Lennon, *Just Like Starting Over* (December 1980; died December 1980)

 Notorious B.I.G., *Hypnotize* (May 1997), *Mo Money Mo Problems* (August 1997; died March 1997)

 Soulja Slim, *Slow Motion* (August 2004; died November 2003)

★ Static Major, *Lollipop* (May 2008; died February 2008)

Ten Fascinating Facts about Elvis Aaron Presley

1 Born Tupelo, Mississippi, January 8, 1935

2 One of twins; his brother, Jesse Garon Presley, died at birth

3 Bought his first guitar in 1946 from the Tupelo Hardware Store (his parents couldn't afford the bike he wanted)

4 Signed his first contract with RCA in 1955

5 Was in 33 films; first was *Love me Tender*, 1956

6   Held a black belt in karate

7   Drafted into US Army in 1958; ID number 53310761; promoted to sergeant in 1960

8   Married Priscilla Beaulieu 1967; divorced 1973

9   Performed last concert June 1977, at Indianapolis Market Square Arena

10   Died August 16, 1977

Elvis Quotes

"I get lonesome sometimes. I get lonesome right in the middle of a crowd."

"Rhythm is either something you have or you don't have, but when you have it, you have it all over."

"I know practically every religious song that's ever been written."

"When music starts, I gotta move."

"You only pass through this life once; you don't come back for an encore."

"Ambition is a dream with a V8 engine."

"I have no use for bodyguards, but I have a very special use for two highly-trained certified public accountants."

"Rock and roll music, if you like it, if you feel it, you can't help move to it. That's what happens to me. I can't help it."

"I want to entertain people. That's my whole life – to my last breath."

"I wanted to be a singer because I didn't want to sweat."

"I don't know anything about music. In my line, you don't have to."

"I hope I haven't bored you."

8

FILM AND TELEVISION

Films with the Highest Box Office Returns

Movie ticket sales only, prices not adjusted for inflation

1	*Titanic* (1997)	$600,779,824
2	*The Dark Knight* (2008)	$528,213,279
3	*Star Wars* (1977)	$460,935,665
4	*Shrek 2* (2004)	$436,471,036
5	*ET* (1982)	$434,949,459
6	*Star Wars: The Phantom Menace* (1999)	$431,065,444
7	*Pirates of the Caribbean: Dead Man's Chest* (2006)	$423,032,628

8	*Spider-Man* (2002)	$403,706,375
9	*Star Wars: Revenge of the Sith* (2005)	$380,262,555
10	*The Lord of the Rings* (2003)	$377,019,252

Top Television Broadcasts since 1964

Estimated number of households

1	*M.A.S.H.* series finale February 1983	50.15 million
2	*Dallas Who Shot JR?* November 1980	41.47 million
3	*Roots* finale January 1977	36.38 million
4	Superbowl XVI San Francisco 49ers v Cincinnati Bengals January 1982	40.02 million
5	Superbowl XVII Washington Redskins v Miami Dolphins January 1983	40.48 million
6	Winter Olympics Ladies' Figure Skating February 1994	45.69 million
7	Superbowl XX Chicago Bears v New England Patriots January 1986	41.49 million

8	Part 1 *Gone with the Wind*	
	November 1976	33.96 million
9	Part 2 *Gone with the Wind*	
	November 1976	33.75 million
10	Superbowl XII Dallas Cowboys v Denver Broncos	
	January 1978	34.41 million

Top Product Placement Brands

Broadcast television; January–July 2008

1   Coca-Cola

2   24-Hour Fitness

3   Chef Revival

4   AT&T

5   Pussycat Dolls Lounge

6   Nike (footwear)

7   Freemotion Fitness

8   Chicago Bears

9   Nike (clothing)

10   Precor

Top Programs for Product Placement

Broadcast television; January–July 2008

★ *American Idol* (Fox)

★ *Biggest Loser* (NBC)

★ *Deal or No Deal* (NBC)

★ *Extreme Makeover Home Edition* (ABC)

★ *Apprentice* (NBC)

★ *Hell's Kitchen* (Fox)

★ *Big Brother* 9 (CBS)

★ *One Tree Hill* (CW)

★ *America's Next Top Model* (CW)

★ *Last Comic Standing* (NBC)

Real Names

Woody Allen	Allen Stewart Konigsberg
Alice Cooper	Vincent Damon Furnier
Joan Crawford	Lucille Fay LeSueur
Tony Curtis	Bernard Schwartz

Kirk Douglas	Issur Danielovitch
Bob Dylan	Robert Allen Zimerman
Carmen Electra	Tara Patrick
Judy Garland	Francis Ethel Gumm
Charlie Sheen	Carlos Estevez
Martin Sheen	Ramon Estevez
Mr. T	Lawrence Tureaud
Bette Davis	Ruth Elizabeth Davis
Nicolas Cage	Nicholas Coppola
Rock Hudson	Roy Scherer

Actors Known by their Middle Names

★ Edward Montgomery Clift

★ Dorothy Faye Dunaway

★ William Clark Gable

★ Norvell Oliver Hardy

★ Terence Steve McQueen

★ Patrick Ryan O'Neal

★ Eldred Gregory Peck

Funny Television Quotes

"It's amazing that the amount of news that happens in the world every day just exactly fits in the newspaper."

Jerry Seinfield

"My husband said he needed more space. So I locked him outside."

Roseanne Barr

"Boy those French. They have a different word for everything!"

Steve Martin

"Here's something to think about: How come you never see a headline like 'Psychic Wins Lottery'?"

Jay Leno

"The New England Journal of Medicine reports that 9 out of 10 doctors agree that 1 out of 10 doctors is an idiot."

Jay Leno

"Today is Valentine's Day, or as men like to call it, Extortion Day!"

Jay Leno

"It's official: Arnold said he will enter the race for governor. At least that's what everyone thinks he said."

David Letterman

"The crime problem in New York is getting really serious. The other day the Statue of Liberty had both hands up."

Jay Leno

"Behind every great man is a woman rolling her eyes."

Jim Carrey

"Gentlemen, start your egos."

Billy Crystal

"I'm not afraid to die. I just don't want to be there when it happens."

Woody Allen

Most Memorable Catchphrases

"Yada, yada, yada."	Jerry Seinfeld, *Seinfeld*
"Eat my shorts."	Bart Simpson, *The Simpsons*
"How you doin'?"	Joey Tribbiani, *Friends*
"Live long and prosper."	Spock, *Star Trek*
"Let's hug it out, bitch."	Ari Gold, *Entourage*
"Come on down."	Johnny Olson and Ron Doddy, *The Price is Right*
"What'choo talkin' 'bout Willis?"	Arnold Drummond, *Diff'rent Strokes*

"Who loves ya, baby?"	Lt Theo Kojak, *Kojak*
"What's up, doc?"	Bugs Bunny, *Looney Tunes*
"Cowabunga!"	*Teenage Mutant Ninja Turtles*
"You're fired!"	Donald Trump, *The Apprentice*
"I pity the fool!"	Mr. T, *The A-Team*
"Let's be careful out there."	Sgt Phil Esterhaus, *Hill Street Blues*
"Aaaaaaayyyyyyyyyy!"	Fonzie, *Happy Days*
"Heeeeeeere's Johnny!"	Ed McMahon, *The Tonight Show*
"D'oh!"	Homer Simpson, *The Simpsons*

Longest-running Series

★ *Meet the Press*, since 1947

★ *CBS Evening News*, since 1948

★ *Today*, since 1952

★ *Guiding Light*, since 1952

★ *Hallmark Hall of Fame*, since 1952 (not continuous)

★ *World News*, since 1953

★ *The Tonight Show*, since 1954

★ *Face The Nation*, since 1954

★ *As the World Turns*, since 1956

★ *NBC Nightly News*, since 1956

The Emmys

★ Most wins: *Frasier* (37)

★ Most nominations: *ER* (122)

★ Actor with most wins: Carl Reiner (9)

★ Actresses with most wins: Cloris Leachman, Mary Tyler Moore, and Tracey Ullman (7)

★ Most individual wins: James Brooks and Edward Greene (19)

★ Most individual nominations: Jac Venza (57)

★ Most wins in a single season: *The West Wing* (9) – its first season

★ Most wins by a network in a single season: CBS (44)

Most wins for a drama series: *Hill Street Blues*, *LA Law*, and *The West Wing* (4)

 Most nominations for a drama series: *NYPD Blue* (27)

The Oscars

 Official name is "Academy Award of Merit"

 Statuette is 13½ inches tall; model of a knight holding a sword, standing on a film reel

 Around 3,000 statuettes have been awarded since 1929

 Statuettes take three to four weeks to make

 During World War II, statuettes were made of plaster as part of the war effort

 Youngest person ever to receive an Oscar – Shirley Temple (five years old) in 1934 – honorary Oscar

 Youngest ever full recipient – Tatum O'Neill (ten years old)

 Person awarded most Oscars – Walt Disney (26)

 Highest number of nominations (actress) – Meryl Streep (15)

★ Highest number of nominations (actor) – Jack Nicholson (12)

★ Most wins (actress) – Katharine Hepburn (4)

★ Most wins (actor) – Jack Nicholson and Walter Brennan (3)

Bob Hope Quotes

"I grew up with six brothers. That's how I learned to dance - waiting for the bathroom."

"A bank is a place that will lend you money if you can prove that you don't need it."

"A James Cagney love scene is one where he lets the other guy live."

"A sense of humor is good for you. Have you ever heard of a laughing hyena with heartburn?"

"Bigamy is the only crime where two rites make a wrong."

"If you watch a game, it's fun. If you play it, it's recreation. If you work at it, it's golf."

"Middle age is when your age starts to show around your middle."

"She said she was approaching forty, and I couldn't help wondering from what direction."

"I don't feel old. I don't feel anything till noon. That's when it's time for my nap."

"I have a wonderful make-up crew. They're the same people restoring the Statue of Liberty."

Stars who Worked in Soap Operas

Christopher Walken, *Guiding Light* (1952)

Alec Baldwin, *The Doctors* (1963)

Morgan Freeman, *Another World* (1964)

Tom Berenger, *One Life to Live* (1968)

Laurence Fishburne, *One Life to Live* (1968)

Sigourney Weaver, *Somerset* (1970)

Tommy Lee Jones, *One Life to Live* (1971)

Kevin Bacon, *Search for Tomorrow* (1979), *Guiding Light* (1980)

Tom Selleck, *The Young and the Restless* (2001)

Former Professions

Calista Flockhart   Aerobics instructor

Bruce Willis	Bartender
Tom Hanks	Bellboy
Jerry Springer	Mayor of Cincinnati
Charles Bronson	Coalminer
Denzel Washington	Coffin polisher
Whoopi Goldberg	Funeral parlor make-up artist
Norm MacDonald	Garbage collector
Jim Carrey	Janitor
Jay Leno	Mechanic
Quentin Tarantino	Video-store clerk
David Letterman	Weatherman
Sylvester Stallone	Lion-cage cleaner
Warren Beatty	Rat catcher

Television Pets

★ Mr Ed (*Mister Ed*)

★ Trigger (*Roy Rogers*)

★ Lassie (*Lassie*)

★ Flipper (*Flipper*)

★ Dino the Dinosaur (*The Flintstones*)

★ Snoopy (*Charlie Brown*)

★ Scooby-Doo (*Scooby-Doo*)

★ Marcel (*Friends*)

★ Salem (*Sabrina the Teenage Witch*)

★ Santa's Little Helper (*The Simpsons*)

Iconic Movie Quotes

"Frankly, my dear, I don't give a damn."
Clark Gable as Rhett Butler in
Gone with the Wind

"I'm going to make him an offer he can't refuse."
Marlon Brando as Vito Corleone
in *The Godfather*

"Here's looking at you, Kid."
Humphrey Bogart as Rick Blaine in *Casablanca*

"Go ahead, make my day."
Clint Eastwood as Harry Callahan
in *Sudden Impact*

"May the force be with you."
Harrison Ford as Han Solo in *Star Wars*

"You talking to me?"
Robert de Niro as Travis Bickle in *Taxi Driver*

"ET phone home."
> Pat Walsh as ET in *ET: the Extra-Terrestial*

"Made it, Ma. Top of the world."
> James Cagney as Arthur "Cody" Jarret
> in *White Heat*

"You can't handle the truth!"
> Jack Nicholson as Col Nathan Jessep
> in *A Few Good Men*

"You're gonna need a bigger boat."
> Roy Scheider as Martin Brody in *Jaws*

"I'll be back."
> Arnold Schwarzenegger as The Terminator
> in *The Terminator*

"Mama always said life was like a box of chocolates. You never know what you're gonna get."
> Tom Hanks as Forrest Gump in *Forrest Gump*

"Houston, we have a problem."
> Tom Hanks as Jim Lovell in *Apollo 13*

"Yo, Adrian!"
> Sylvester Stallone as Rocky Balboa in *Rocky*

"I feel the need – the need for speed!"
> Tom Cruise and Anthony Edwards
> as Maverick and Goose in *Top Gun*